PRAISE FOR HEATHER BELL

The only thing lonelier than being alone is loving the wrong person. Bell's collection taps into that space, that lack of space, the power of love to spay. When it turns to hate, we might wonder whether or not it was really love in the first place, and we might die wondering. But *Regret or Something More Animal* gives us hope for the wounded dove, all swan songs aside, and the opportunity to reclaim our hearts and minds. "I am reminded that women writers can eat you alive," says Bell, and I, too, am reminded.

— KIM VODIKA, AUTHOR OF *THE ELVIS MACHINE*

T0273755

Heather Bell's *Regret or Something More Animal* devastates the reader with a field guide to the dissolution of marriage and new life in its shadow. Her poems trace the boundaries of maternal guilt, sexual violence, and love, tenderly exposing their bones in fresh metaphors and bright images. Airy and organic, Bell's phrases invite the reader into a world haunted by birds, frogs and willows, and punctuated with cigarettes, suicide and real trauma. All the while, Bell sings us through the pain of failure and fear in romance and wings us toward survival's questions about what it takes to love the shattered self before it is mended.

— DAPHNE MAYSONET, CO-FOUNDER OF THE CORNER CLUB

Heather Bell's *Regret or Something More Animal* is a riveting and revealing collection on how this poet not only survived a divorce but has taken the pain and crafted the experience into such empowering poems like "You Are Animal Too." My favorite poem is "All Misogyny removed, Notes from My Husband." Despite all the parts redacted by Bell, the words she left reflect her fearlessly piercing eloquence, that will leave you stung on and off page. You will even will feel reverberations like this long after reading each of Heather's verses. The best poets like Bell expose so much that we can see ourselves, our current and past relationships glaring back at us from poems like "Look at the Way You Behave" that you experience on the page. You will never love a poetry collection like this again. Discovering the aching beauty of "Something I Will Probably Never Say to You" is a verse we would all want to share with a former flame that has burned us in our past. Bell's poems not only connect they leave teeth marks and you will savor each line that she tattoos around your skin. What I loved most about poems like "Old Age," "Hotel" and "Prone to Aggression" is that Heather Bell universal voice shows how although we are fragile, we have primal animalistic qualities that ooze through such ferociously memorable poems that you will make you want to devour *Regret or Something More Animal* again and again.

— ADRIAN ERNESTO CEPEDA,
AUTHOR OF *LA BELLE AJAR*

The contemplation of Regret or Something More Animal creates a liminal space, where the speaker becomes more aware of the horror the heart endures, specifically theirs, in an attempt to re-define what love is & re-mend that which has been contorted by years of abuse. The very first line opens the entire premise of this book with, "What's interesting about the / human heart is the horror of it," examining the wearing lacerations the heart endures, while preparing us [readers] for a metaphorical surgery that must remove the heart & disembowel it, in order to place the pieces back together. But, no matter what, it will never be the same as it was. Love will never be the same (each time). In Regret or Something More Animal Heather journeys through the heart's many ventricles, analyzing the architecture of the effects of abusive love & blissful love, & everything in between. The speaker says, "A wound can't close itself..." & so they attempt to find some suture through experience & re-definition, with the journey itself becoming the true destination.

— COURTNEY LEIGH, AUTHOR OF
THE UNREQUITED <3<3 OF RED
RIDING HOOD & HER LYCAN LOVER

Heather Bell takes out the wedding dress and feeds it to the wood chipper, with grace and without any traces of mascara running down her face. Bell asks the question we all weep over: *how will I ever love again?* and then takes us from the breakdown to the breakthrough. "I step back quickly as you do when a caged thing moves," Bell writes; be ready to stay quick on your feet.

REGRET OR SOMETHING MORE ANIMAL

HEATHER BELL

CL◢SH

Copyright © 2020 by Heather Bell

ISBN: 978-1-944866-63-1

Cover by Joel Amat Güell

CLASH Books

clashbooks.com

Email: clashmediabooks@gmail.com

This book could not have happened without a divorce, booze, many house plants and a human grizzly bear named Dan Atkinson.

Thank you for picking me up off the floor when I was difficult and weeping.

You remember too much,
    my mother said to me recently.
    Why hold onto all that? And I said,
    Where can I put it down?

                        — ANNE CARSON, GLASS, IRONY
                                    AND GOD

YOU ARE ANIMAL TOO

What's interesting about the
human heart is the horror of it.
The pulsing, the sloppy blood.
Did he know about the seagull
cawing at my heart chest before he said

I think maybe I might
love you

as a bandage loves to
press and press on a scab's top.

I think perhaps
I may love you even though
the wind is so strong

picked me up and
pulled me away for awhile.

It is a rumor that the human
heart is a matte pink, flat
and weird, stingray of the body.

The problem is the investigation
before the opening of your chest:

you think maybe there is a small
peninsula of ugly, maybe just at
the tip of the meaty organ. How else

do humans keep loving? There is
no way the heart could be so
disastrous to see. And yet,

the garment of my love has
fallen and I have nothing left
to give you: here it is

the hunger and the bruises,
the clouds and the train
song clattering through the muscle

as if to say I am animal
but you
are animal too.

OCTOPUS SEX

A male octopus has a specialized
sex arm which allows him to mate
with a female from a distance. This is

similar to human beings in that,
it sounds sexy. Imagine, you see
your partner from across the room, across
the street, miles away even. You like

him but let's be honest: the human male

is the mannequin of mammals. Sex
barely moving, blanket old and itchy,
blank stares. But sex for an octopus

seems like freedom. Give me
your dick from light years away,

who needs the sweaty thrust and
oh god let it be over. In the pacific

somewhere a glittery female barely

changes her day. The flesh a quick

shooting star then gone. Ah, I love you,
my tentacles would be so perfect in
an embrace but I have no time

for you my darling,
create in absence,
never touch.

AFTER THE STORM

At that moment after the storm
I asked the universe
for a sign that this was the risk
worth risking

and the sky looked sort of gray,
very normal for a sky
after so much rain

and I knew you would
never love me the way I wanted
but after a storm there is always
a calmness
like after the sob
when you know what you have to do.

RUNNING AWAY IS NEVER
SIMPLE

you cannot find your red suitcase,
the one with the gold around it
like a picture frame
of blood. What to bring? Not the books,

leave those. Bring things to keep you
human: lipstick, five pairs of shoes,
pet frog in an old mason jar. Because
you will leave and then the fur

begins and the snarl. The deep growl
buried at the ears. You will be driving
and all the love in the world is gone
and you begin weeping but also
the howl. Why have you left,
turn around, pull over, what are you

doing, running into the woods. What
was it that kept you normal,
upright? Was it your husband's angry

love, washing his old t shirts until they
have holes and then you wear them to bed

because they have his mossy scent?
Was it the way he pulled your arm back
and you closed your eyes knowing
it will be over soon, just grit your teeth,

you are doing fine? In the woods you

allow the strangeness to come, touch
your teeth to trees as if to say
this is freedom,
primitive, weird. Marriage has been

the hawk at the top of the tree
calling down

"I am waiting for you to give up"

and you replying
but I can be stronger, the wingspan
of my heart is better
I can do this

You limp back to your car
You go home
your eyebrows are just eyebrows again,
your hands no longer
ferocious.

PRONE TO AGRESSION

I tell him where I want
to go to graduate school and he
says maybe
you should think about
universities that aren't so

prestigious and I say oh,
I think I am ready and he laughs

so pace the floor and
my editor says sure
we can publish that piece
titled, "His Tiny Penis
Satisfies No Woman,"

and I am reminded
that women writers
can eat you alive

HEATHER BELL

like a labradoodle
that learns — you think
it is stupid

when all you were waiting for

was love from him,
so you bite, latch onto the face,
throw his head back and forth

and no one will believe it
because you're a labradoodle
and those sorts of dogs
don't bite

HE IS UNDERNEATH MY CAR IN THE GARAGE

fixing my brakes. He says, "can you hand
me that wrench?" and I know then that
I will never love anyone again. He is

grunting like he's skinning a fox
or bear. It is September and I will never

love anyone again. I will not cry about it.

My heart has a face and it is covered
in wounds so love has become too
dangerous. It is September, I count twelve
weird singing orioles in the tree. He barks,

"I need the hammer, woman!" and I idly
wonder what it is like to be loved,
the way the water at the lake loves
driftwood. The way the waves place it

on the shore but then returns to softly
take it home. I no longer want to run away,

even, because all homes become
violent eventually. I turn my back
to the garage and whisper, "I will never

love anyone again" and I let there
be a wail underneath the small words.
It is okay, here is your wrench, hammer,
battered bits of sheetrock saved in my
nightstand, from when you hit the wall
when you meant to hit me. Because

there is no one in this world willing
to love me, it is September, time blows
by like an ambulance siren. He says,
"bitch give me the wrench again!" Ok,
I reply calmly even though my life is

geese migrating. I will never love anyone
again, I am too small and sad and tired.
I sit on the gravel driveway, quietly
listening for what he needs next.

WOMANHOOD

She says, "does any of this
scare you," and oh, it does. The
blue-green Leningrad of her hair.
The time she was at my house
and each time she walked past:

the scent of anxiety, ketchup,
literature. But the kind of books,
specifically that anger you
at the end. Because why did the
main character not realize
how beautiful she was at the waist
and ankle? And how could her lover

let years roll through their bodies
without falling in love? "I am afraid

of nothing," I reply. Because what else

can I say? She may think me crazy

if I say I am afraid to stand silently
with her at a kitchen window and want
her to hold my hand but she does not.

They say love is about the little things:

a woman's calf where there has been
no leg by mine at all. Finding hairs in
my bed that are not my own. In the

dimming light when I imagine her
saying "I am not beautiful," and I

laugh until I realize she is
serious and I hold her
wondering what has life done?

SEX LIVES

When I am around other women
I ask them about their sex lives
in order to create order in my life.
One woman claws at his neck
another woman says she turns away
and waits patiently like a small thin
bird for it to be over so she can
do what she really wants: which is

eat the leftovers: tulips she cooked
in gelatin. The last woman always

lies and says her human feet move
her to his human body and they
make love, as humans do. Her upper

arms dotted in bruises, little henpecks
of mystery. I tell her that

this city has twelve thousand four
hundred and sixty people. Maybe one
or two will huddle with you while you
weep after telling the truth. Later

that night she says yeah he rapes me
but whatever because what else is there?

Besides rape, I think? Besides men or
mortgages? Dandelions weren't always

considered a weed, I say. I stop talking
when she snorts up the air
like a circus elephant and I
step back quickly as you do when a caged thing
suddenly moves.

A WAY TO RELEASE ENERGY

That's what gardening is, she said. No
one *really* enjoys gardening.
Hydrangeas = dead children. Tomatoes = abusive
husbands.
The worst is when you spend hours constructing a
raised bed garden and
the best fertilizer is laid and each seed is exactly six
inches away

from the next seed. And it doesn't matter.
Carrots = terrible loss.
Geraniums = perpetually dirty carpets.
Lilac = awkward sex conversations.

The universe blows through
right after a woodchuck unearths each sprout
and leaves it

as it is disappointing. And the air and atoms rustle around
and the corn is mixed with arugula is mixed with
peppers, etc, she says,

and she looks very sad because arugula is for the
time she was molested and
of course peppers are children
facing a wall. Weeks go by and you get
clumps of this and that:
beans strangling everything like skinny rapists.

She said, this is why I am so sad
and I say, oh.

WRITE THIS DOWN

I have killed before, she says. Chickens, you
can just snap the neck. Hogs, something sharp is
needed. Once we had a turkey and I used a .22.

Three times, human babies. Mine.

Yours, I say and she nods and her hair looks
like a rooftop, shaved to the root.

I say, I wanted to talk to you so you could tell me
about death but I thought you would talk about
your own. I am 17 and this woman is being
interviewed

for my school paper. Late stage brain cancer. Pal-
liative care,
hospice, something. Tell me something about

yourself, I think. But she starts murmuring
that there were three separate circumstances in
which

she did not want to be a mother. And now?

I still do not want to be a mother, don't be an idiot,
she says. There is a moon shaped scar in three posi-
tions on

her head. Like some sort of galaxy. I want her to

tell me about the surgeries. I want to know
each time

it didn't work. I want to know what the doctors
wore
and if they had black hair, red hair, blonde
as drought-grass. You see, she says,

you're looking for what isn't important. I did not
love these children,
I did not love anything. Do I still? I loved the way
my husband's face

looked like a crumpled tuxedo at a wedding when
they said I was dying.
I loved that my house looked like a mannequin
head when I came home, the

first time. Looking at me, no expression. But
windows for eyes,
unmoving, dead. Look at me, little girl,

does anyone ever see a body bag except on tv or if
you are
investigating a crime? Not regular people. We see
the fancy
caskets, inlaid with cherry blossoms. I wanted
to say

-get me out of here-
but she reached for my shoulder and pressed down
hard and said
feel that? You'll never feel that again,
in just that same way, from a woman with no hair.
 Buck up, buttercup,

just write this down,
grief melts that way,
write this down.

THE WEEPING

For the nine years I was married,
whenever I would cry
my husband would leave or

argue the hurt in
further. Yesterday,

I hid in my blankets
and sobbed

I felt the mattress
move with your weight and
you quietly said
don't cry

like it was a real choice
and you ran your hands over
my back and your breath

was cigarettes and black coffee
your sweatshirt was laundry detergent
and everything you have ever fixed
you said "what

is wrong?" Nothing
my garter snake surprising me
in low grass. Nothing

my crow on the windowsill watching
me ache in the morning. Nothing

is wrong now, beautiful eyes like
the Blue Gray Tanager I saw

singing at the tree top and I
thought oh, you must be lost,

but you kept singing
as if you knew how badly
I needed that song.

THE BEARD

The gray hairs at your ears,
I say "old man," and you say,
"Hush, angel." We met and I
loved your coffee scent, old cigarettes,
Sadness. I loved you immediately,
neck tattoo to cover the name
of an ex. A bird. Wingspan.
 From one tip of the heart to
the other. Your ex, she says I am

dirty for not knowing you well enough
before wanting to pretzel my heart
with yours. But how long does it take

to know your person belongs only
to you? I had been married 9 years,
divorced one day and you
held me at the mouth with your

hands shhh it's okay to feel this.

if there is no one else to love you,
then it will be my job because I am

not very good at it but i will always
try. your mustache sucking into your
mouth, perfect. Your gray eyes, like
The color I wanted to paint my dining
room walls but did not, yes. The reason

I am weeping is because of this: your
quiet sleep snorts at 5am. The way you
held my hands when we made love. That

you said you needed to know why I was
sad. No reason anymore, just keep me

like a weird animal in a cage, who
should want to be free but the door is

not locked and still
I sit here and wait for you.

AGE

"I'm too old for this," I whisper
to myself. Because love, well,

I was married nine years. After
that long you know what love is:

the time my husband asked me
to butcher the quail and I got
so confused as to how that I used
kitchen scissors. And their tiny bodies

shuddered the life out as I said,
"I am sorry." That's what I thought love

was and now oh, what if it's not?

Because my heart is upside down
for someone, oh I want to roost

at his neck. I tell the story of my

marriages failure and he knows I
am not talking about a failure of love,
but how does he know that, how

to know that I had no idea what
love even is, still do not. It's almost

February, but mild so I walk slowly to

the back of the property and I see
a small game bird and it looks at me

and I notice the way it has no fear
because it is free, because
this is its home.

HOTEL

"I was married for nine years," I cough
like marriage is a sickness or
gets stuck in the lungs. And after it
ended, I started sleeping on our
old green couch, with the pattern
of weeping willows. I ask you to
sleep next to me in a hotel because

there is a spot there, dusk shadowing
the wrinkle. And you say ok even though

"I was married for nine years, and I failed
at all nine," I say. I ask you to sleep next

to me in a hotel because the flowering
dogwood of your hair. The marrow

at your neck, the scent of mountain lion,
crushed flowers, sadness.

"I was married for nine years, I think,"
I want to cry. You say, "come here," but

I am already there.

IN ANOTHER LIFETIME

I was a grocery store clerk
and you asked me where
the shampoo was located
and I did not know so I said
"go past the florist section and
turn right by the eggs,"
and I wanted to say, but wait,
something is familiar about you:

you're the reason I am here,
or anywhere. You are the feeling
of sobbing and the someone appears
with outstretched arms. You walked

away and I remembered being
in a museum and they turned the
lights off and on the ceiling
there were thousands of LED pin pricks

which were supposed to make us
feel at peace to see: stars but not,

like a bee hive I saw once in an artist's
studio, made of glass. You,

other lifetime you, alternate dimension
you, you with maybe a different

mustache, fluffier or unkempt,
who knows. You did not return

and I imagine you found the shampoo
or found someone more intelligent
and beautiful to help you
find what you needed. That night

another lifetime me
dreamt of
another lifetime you
and we

sat in my garden and I placed
squash blossoms in your beard
because it was funny or because

this lifetime might be the one
where we do not fall in love,
so I tell you the story of when I was
six and we visited the ocean

and I spent all day making a huge
sandcastle and not one person told
me it was too close to the water
to survive. But it was
so exquisite, sea shell windows and

clear sea glass door knobs. No one
wanted to stop me, even though
it would never last. But you never know

exactly how far the tide will come in,
and when I ran to the water the next
morning, it was there: sandy spires
and stick flags, triumphant.

WHORL

I lied and said
I had not seen you
at the supermarket
because I was on my way
to buy more jam jars
and I knew you would make
me forget
about the jam jars
about everything
even my own heart

So I do the thing
I do when I am nervous
repeat words I find difficult to
pronounce: forsythia, chrysanthemum,
whorl, spathe. I walk away quickly

hoping you didn't see the hitch

in my bones: like a lab skeleton
being pieced together and hung.

I got twelve jam jars, crackers,
a plastic package of white bread
and I was crying in my truck

outside the supermarket
these are things two people
never confess to each other:

maybe I could have lived
without the jam jars,
maybe I shouldn't have slid
so artfully away.

MY GRANDMOTHER
HATED MEN

My grandmother never liked my
husband, but she would have loved you.
She would have said, "that man's heart
is a duffel bag filled with creatures

like the frogs you keep in the summer
in a big aquarium in your kitchen. The
three legged turtles found
in the road and you worried

they would never find love
now that they weren't perfect
anymore." My grandmother hated men,

but she would have loved you:
the color of your beard,
her favorite. The one time she showed
me a picture with a man

with a bird sitting on his head
and she laughed and laughed- "marry
up," she said and drank more
vodka. My grandmother, she hated

all men, knew the trouble of them:

the way they bend your heart
backwards, just enough to make you
weep for years. But, I think,

she would have loved you,
your eyes like the Atlantic at low tide,
planets, the blue forgiveness

at a bird's neck. "Because love is
gentle," she said, to explain why

men were dangerous. Oh, she would
have loved you, held your hands,
admitted she was wrong,
while you ate her buttered toast like
a son or the feral cat she kept

that everyone was afraid of but
she knew just needed to be held.

ALL MISOGYNY REMOVED,
NOTES FROM MY HUSBAND

Your hair [redacted]. My warmth, feel the
[redacted]
sadness. [redacted]. At my house, with wild
turkeys, we [redacted]. What I really mean is:

have you [redacted] much lately? Have you
pressed a
large seashell to your [redacted]? Would you
ever walk

with me, wearing only one boot and a [redacted]
and
cloisonne necklace and I would [redacted] all over
your

[redacted]. This wasn't meant to be offensive but

can I maybe touch [redacted] or nourish you with
soup when
you are sick or just [redacted]? Can I take you to
the hospital

after I [redacted] and there is nothing left where
your
[redacted] should be? Haha fuck you, cunt,
I can love too, I matter [redacted]. I have a
heart too,
you know, [redacted].

LOOK AT THE WAY YOU BEHAVE

He says he took a bunch of uppers once
to kill himself and I know
I will fall in love with this man

just like how I could feel the slow
tumble of my marriage, like a

taraxacum officinalis, dead and
spreading seeds. My husband says, "you don't

know what love is, look at the way
you behave." I am embarrassed of

my own heart.   I will fall in love

with *this* man, not my husband,
who so artfully broke me
like a horse,

or china plate. This is the man

that may or may not
be dangerous lilac,
the poaching of a heart. And I say

if you ever feel that way again,
please tell me
we can sit under a heavy blanket
and weep. Until night and stars and stars

please don't leave me ever,
I say. I mean it, you know,
pretty beard, deadly gull singing
at the base of a mountain:

I need you.

DICTATOR

Eyebrows, Russian dictator
mustache, everything I should
say but did not. Such as: your knee is

touching mine lightly, please
move closer. I like your hair color,

the shade of leaves during autumn
and the desperate fruit attached. Such

as: does your mouth taste like saltwater,
a place I was in 2008, California, too cold
to swim but I did anyway. Such as: your skin,
your eyes like when you are drowning

in inches of water, just pretending to die
for the thrill of it. Lastly, but maybe not:

the moons of your nail beds, I looked
at secretly while you spoke and thought

about holding your hands, pulling them
up to my chest as if they were weeping
and my heart was a place to hold
the tears.

YOUR COCK

beautiful as
the harmonica I bought on a whim at
twenty-three. I also bought a book to learn
to play, but instead I did the wrong thing
and loved the wrong person.

For years,
loved the wrong person. I am so sorry,
the harmonica, I carried it with me
through every heartbreak,
but never touched. Is this what real love

is? to place your sex in a box sadly
each time you left and then begin again?

Forgive me, I should have known
you were always with me,

now come to me
in me
never leave.

I DO NOT LIKE WINTER

I do not like winter because
Of its small bones. Like a rat, dormouse,
chinchilla. There appears callouses
in my palms from the firewood hauling.
My son wakes up quickly in winter,
night terrors.

I mean that the air is delicate. It has been
ten years now and my marriage is
a ghost. I am my own flashlight

in winter. I am alone to hold a lamp
as my husband sleeps. Ten years,

weak bones, brittle like that of a
dead thing buried then dragged
to the surface. In winter, I begin a
friendship with a strange man.

By February it was over, my husband
accuses me of adultery. It was
something, not that, but I agree to say
affair just as someone agrees to dessert
after a big meal. Because why not?

My husband does all sorts of things
to me with his rage. My children sit
quietly reading a dictionary,
pointing at different words and trying to
say them:

femur
flagellate
finally

The ice cracks at the window and we
All turn to watch it. Thinking how
Can we fix this and realizing
We don't need to do anything.

I AM THE MOTHER OF TWO
CHILDREN LIVE AND
THREE DEAD

So you live in a tiny house, entirely dependent on
wood heat in the winter. Let's say you live some-
where cold. Alaska. The North Pole. Neptune.
 Let's say you run out of logs to burn. Maybe you
were too lazy to cut the appropriate amount,
maybe you just miscalculated. But now, what do
you start with? What do you burn first? First
chairs, useless wooden bowls from your grand-
mother. Then it's January and you're sitting on the
floor so what next? The legs of your sofa, maybe
the headboard of your bed. There's only

so much burnable inside a house. Before long you
look at your dog. Panic. Look at your husband.
 Cry. Your first born, just the right size. Your left
arm, who needs it? There's only so much. You try
going out there,

waist deep snow, weeping through it. All you have
is an old maul. You're exhausted, aren't you? What
more can you give up, throw into the fire?

You know it's only you or the house left, the old
lathe would spark like nothing, like it was meant to.
 But you can only sit outside a burning house

for so long before it's just a hill of black and you're
cold again and pawing through the ash like a hungry
animal oh no, this does not smell like something
that could sustain you through February. Because
there's a limit to what you

you can burn. The mistake is always what you
choose to start with.

SOMETHING I WILL PROBABLY
NEVER SAY TO YOU

I love you, sea creature,
hair dark like amber tea steeped too long.
I love you like a lost person
in the woods in winter
loves the matches in her pocket
I love you, strange funny bird,
I imagine your neck feels like
maybe rough sadness or
the sharp edges of a metal roof
I want to say no you can never leave
once you are here but will you
ever be here, who knows,

I stand at the wire fence
which is a good place to sob
I love you like an umbrella
who believes she is human
and you know that

No one else has ever known that
or wanted to know

This is the thing you are not supposed
to admit: I love you,
I love you, I love you,
my wet star with a voice like a weapon

Maybe I will someday have the courage
to show you this poem
maybe not

HOW TO SURVIVE A NUCLEAR APOCALYPSE

After awhile, the curtain drops dramatically
on your rage. After awhile: does it matter

anymore once you have found your freedom?
At 5am every morning
they wake us to get vitals. 98.6, blood

pressure normal, heart still seems to
be thumping away. In the facility I read

instructional booklets on how to play
a mandolin. How to crochet. How to
survive a nuclear apocalypse. After awhile

I realize of course there is no mandolin
to hold against my hand. There cannot be

crochet rods because they are a danger

to our lives. And although it suggests
I collect canned goods, I have
no cans. Isn't that the way it always is:

you can think you know how to
do a certain thing but you are always

missing an important part. The nurse
checks my mouth that I swallowed my
medication and I say thank you because
after awhile the rage no longer matters,

you take what you can to survive
even if it's not
what you need. No legs when you
need to run. No sadness when a patient
tells their own suicide story. What is left?

I open my mouth and say thank you
lift my tongue, show the spaces around
my teeth

thank you.

SHE SAID, "DON'T WAIT, JUST GO"

A wound can't close itself,
or at least not the kind we are
talking about. I think deeply and
quietly of my grandmother
who also loved two men. How
they would vacation to the ocean
and my grandmother would let
the washed up jellyfish sting
her hands over and over
until she cried. But now, I'm 34,
married with two kids and

I understand that craving for pain.
She says: I once lost my sandals
at the river and had to walk over
these sharp stones and glass
barefoot. It's like that for you, too,
right? I mean, you'll eventually

make it to the soft grass of shore
but you will be bleeding by the time
you get there. Don't wait,

just go, she says again. But
I am wearing my sadness as a helmet
and the roar echoes only back to me
inside, and I don't think I will ever

go, isn't that easier, safer?
She says: don't wait, just go
and she's eating a nectarine
angrily like maybe she feels regret
or something more animal.

GIVING UP

It is with deep sadness that goodbye. I have held
on to you for too long. The crash of you, suddenly
into bed. So stock market. So dead bird. So heart
attack. The showerdamp hair, the blue jean crinkle.
I have a deep sadness so goodbye. Because when
trauma. Trauma. What yes a deep sadness. A deep
sadness. Around 2009, I tried killing myself. Not
very important details but relevant to the story so
keep listening. There was a skirt

patterned in open windows. This would be funnier
in Morse code because dot dot dash I tried to kill
myself dot dash. After you become a mother. After
you have a great heron rise from your body. After
you hear a song

of which there are no other songs to compare. A
mother. You know that the sadness has to say

goodbye. Because there is a diligence in a mother's
work. Bend, pulled to breast with cloth, tied.
 Because after the blood I whispered

I will be there for you. There is the story of the
Great Mother who destroyed worlds all with her
children strapped to her back with cloth made
of stars. There is that. You know my grandmother
did not have this, this moment to say goodbye. To
the rage. The selfish guilt. The sea of disgust

on a man's face as he calls you pig. She birthed
eleven children, one dead and

I am sure she tried to kill herself. I am sure. This
knowledge is in the way

she would tip her cup of gin in the evening. The
saliva at the lip. I do now

what I have to do so goodbye. Goodbye to the
rage, the field of juniper that is my past. The
distant hills are trees and with that I have some-
thing new to burn.

RELAX, WOUND CARE IS HERE

The divorce had been
sitting by your ears until it dripped
in. Like when you cry and cry
while laying like a corpse
on your couch and the tears

they start flowing into
both ear drums
from the gravity of it. Like rivers.

Like sadness. A girl on a boat
with no sail. But still,

there had been love
at some point. And

nothing replaces it. So anyway

there are spots to set the love,
places that need it. And even though

it will never be the same
and there will always be weeping
maybe for years,

you can go to your place,
set more love there,
set more love there,
more love

never less,
and the crying continues
but so does the love.

WHILE YOU SLEEP

I pull lightly on your beard and
your snores change
at each tug
like I'm playing a
song. You grumble and
I am quiet
so as not to wake
such a beautiful thing. Sometimes,
I also whisper to you
things I am still afraid to say
and pretend the hitch in your breath
is agreement.

ACKNOWLEDGMENTS

Thank you to CLASH and specifically Leza Cantoral for believing in me, when I no longer believed in myself. Because life can be an eggplant sometimes. And although you love eggplant, you are a man with no hands.

Thank you Leza for having hands.

ABOUT THE AUTHOR

Heather Bell has been published in numerous literary magazines and journals. She won the 2009 New Letters Prize and in the 2016 Rattle Chapbook Prize, her chapbook "Kill the Dogs" was selected and published. She lives on Oswego, NY with her grizzly bear Dan, 4 human children and 1 prairie dog. She is an assistant teacher in a Montessori school and loves eating rye bread.

Email her at schimelhr@gmail.com

Follow her on IG @bellhr

TRAGEDY QUEENS: STORIES INSPIRED BY LANA DEL REY & SYLVIA PLATH

Edited by Leza Cantoral

GIRL LIKE A BOMB

Autumn Christian

CENOTE CITY

Monique Quintana

HEXIS

Charlene Elsby

99 POEMS TO CURE WHATEVER'S WRONG WITH YOU OR CREATE THE PROBLEMS YOU NEED

Sam Pink

THIS BOOK IS BROUGHT TO YOU BY MY STUDENT LOANS

Megan J. Kaleita

PAPI DOESN'T LOVE ME NO MORE

Anna Suarez

ARSENAL/SIN DOCUMENTOS

Francesco Levato

I'M FROM NOWHERE

Lindsay Lerman

HEAVEN IS A PHOTOGRAPH

Christine Sloan Stoddard

FOGHORN LEGHORN

Big Bruiser Dope Boy

TRY NOT TO THINK BAD THOUGHTS

Art by Matthew Revert

DARK MOONS RISING IN A STARLESS NIGHT

Mame Bougouma Diene

IF YOU DIED TOMORROW I WOULD EAT YOUR CORPSE

Wrath James White

HORROR FILM POEMS

Poetry by Christoph Paul & Art by Joel Amat Güell

NIGHTMARES IN ECSTASY

Brendan Vidito

WE PUT THE LIT IN LITERARY

CLASHBOOKS.COM

FOLLOW US

IG, TWITTER @clashbooks

www.ingramcontent.com/pod-product-compliance
Lightning Source LLC
Jackson TN
JSHW081332130125
77033JS00014B/536